PUT BABY JESUS IN YOUR WAGON

Cover Photo: Shutterstock
Art Director: Karen Knutson
Design Team: Diane Cook, Pamela Dunn

All Scripture quotations, unless otherwise indicated, are taken from the Holy Bible, New International Version®, NIV®. Copyright © 1973, 1978, 1984, 2011 by Biblica, Inc.™ Used by permission of Zondervan. All rights reserved worldwide. www.zondervan.com.

The "NIV" and "New International Version" are trademarks registered in the United States Patent and Trademark Office by Biblica, Inc.™

Scripture marked KJV is from the King James Version of the Bible.

All rights reserved. This publication may not be copied, photocopied, reproduced, translated, or converted to any electronic or machine-readable form in whole or in part, except for brief quotations, without prior written approval from the publisher.

Northwestern Publishing House
1250 N. 113th St., Milwaukee, WI 53226-3284
www.nph.net
© 2015 Northwestern Publishing House
Published 2015
Printed in the United States of America
ISBN 978-0-8100-2711-4
ISBN 978-0-8100-2712-1 (e-book)

PUT BABY JESUS IN YOUR WAGON

A COLLECTION OF WARM CHRISTMAS MEMORIES

Written By
John R. Hardison

NORTHWESTERN PUBLISHING HOUSE
Milwaukee, Wisconsin

REVIEWS

"*Put Baby Jesus in Your Wagon* is a great collection of Christmas stories geared toward encouraging readers to share their Christian faith! John Hardison shows us that the story of Christ's birth can be found in everyday December events. He encourages us to use our Christian faith and our God-given time and talents to serve others at Christmastime and throughout the year."

Mark Westendorf
Chairman
Iron Men of God Men's Conference

"After reading *Put Baby Jesus in Your Wagon*, parents will want to hug their children 'just because' and cherish every moment they have together. Even if you aren't a parent, this book will help you focus on the true meaning of Christmas and teach you what to pray for, especially at Christmas."

Pastor Richard D. Starr
Coordinator
Men Alive! Men's Conference

"I sang along with 'Here Comes Clara Cow'! I snuck into the barn to see the twin calves. I was sitting with the children in the 1922 children's service. I was challenged with my own spirit of giving when I read about mayo and ketchup. Each story is related to God's Word with appropriate applications. *Put Baby Jesus in Your Wagon* is a primer on how Christians can bring that Word to every situation in life."

Pastor Tom Klusmeyer
Director
Camp Phillip, Wautoma, WI

"My first impression of *Put Baby Jesus in Your Wagon* was that it was going to be a collection of heartwarming and poignant memories of Christmases past, but it is more than that! The stories show God's hand in the lives of individuals and bring the focus back to the real reason we celebrate. *Put Baby Jesus in Your Wagon* helped me reflect on the Christmases of my past and the loving way God guided and focused me through those times."

Russ Wagner
Men of His Word Ministries

"It's refreshing to read a book that shares the true meaning of Christmas, which doesn't include magical snowmen, flying reindeer, or men in red suits. This book is a keeper and a wonderful addition to your personal, school, or church library."

Neil Hankwitz
Faith in Action Volunteer Management
Kingdom Workers

DEDICATION

This collection of stories about the celebration of the birth of Jesus is dedicated to the memories of Leo Waldbauer, Don Butler, and Lois McLean, longtime members of Redeemer Lutheran Church in Yakima, Washington. They each loved Christmas, their church, and their Savior. All three of them set a Christian example for all of us who knew them, by demonstrating the full meaning of following in Christ's footsteps at Christmas and throughout the years. I thank God for putting them in my life. I count it a real privilege to have had each of them as a friend.

ABOUT THE AUTHOR

John R. Hardison was born on September 22, 1942. Raised on his folks' citrus, avocado, and cattle ranch located five miles outside the town of Fillmore, California, he worked on his dad and grandparents' ranches doing all kinds of odd jobs. John also found time for horseback riding, hunting, swimming, and hiking. He loved to roam over the acres and acres of ground included in those ranches and the Los Padres National Forest that adjoined his father's ranch.

John attended Whitworth College in Spokane, Washington, from 1960–1964, earning his BA degree. John and his wife moved to Yakima in the fall of 1964 and he became a junior high and high school teacher for the next thirty years, retiring in 1994. His wife also began teaching soon after the birth of their son, Gregory, in the fall of 1964.

He has had to deal with his share of losses in his life. His only son, Gregory, died in an accident in 1977 at age 13. His father died at age 56 of cancer, as did a very close friend from his college years at age 28. More recently his hunting partner of thirty years passed away. John was divorced, but has been happily married to Ruth Friebus Hardison since June 14, 1975.

Ruth and John have spent a lot of time traveling in the western part of the United States and Canada, doing volunteer church work for Redeemer Lutheran Church in Yakima, writing books, horseback riding, hiking, skiing, and hunting. They currently reside in their home on a small ranch ten miles west of Yakima, Washington, where they have horses, dogs, and several cats.

John has written two other books, *Under God's Sky* and *A View From the Mountains*, which are both collections of devotional stories taken from real life events the author or his close friends or relatives have actually lived. You can find out more about his two books and where to get them by visiting www.nph.net.

TABLE OF CONTENTS

Acknowledgments xi

Introduction xiii

1. Put Baby Jesus in Your Wagon 1

2. Asking for Snow 10

3. Babe's Manger 15

4. The Gift* 18

5. Christmas Eve at the Hospital 23

6. Sing-Alongs With Clara and Molly 30

7. A Lesson From a Used Christmas Tree* 39

8. A Season to Remember 43

9. Black Ice 54

10. Sugar Cookies 57

11. Behind the Door 58

12. Christmas Eve — 1922* 67

13. Our Family Christmas Tree 71

14. Stable 76

15. Mayonnaise and Ketchup* 83

16. Christmas Without the Classics 87

17. A Humble Coronation 90

---

*Reprinted from my previous books

ACKNOWLEDGMENTS

Ruth Hardison — My loving wife since we were married on June 14, 1975. She has been a tremendous help in writing this book. She read each article several times. We spent many an hour going over each one of these stories. She suggested corrections and additional ideas to include in many of them. I could not have written this without her loving support.

Don Fluaitt — He volunteered his time to take many of the photographs in this book. I think he did a fantastic job. I am in his debt for all his fine work.

Don Butler — He was an expert on Martin Luther and could tell you just about anything you might want to know about him. Don read my stories and made many suggestions and corrections. His input was extremely helpful. He went to be with the Lord he loved on October 6, 2013. I miss him as a friend and every time I write another story.

Pastor Tim Schwartz — He read most of the articles included in this book. He made many good suggestions and tried his best to help me use just the right words in the right places. I thank him.

Gail and Dona Thornton — Gail is the rancher in many of my stories and a close friend. He has come a long way from when I first saw him sitting as a student in my very first seventh grade class to being a very successful cattle rancher in the Yakima Valley. He was only nine years younger than I in that classroom. Gail and his wife, Dona, continue to encourage me. They often have suggestions and corrections that really improve my work. I appreciate their friendship and their help. Over the years Gail has allowed me to use several events that happened on his ranch and in his life as material for my stories, one of which is included in this book. In addition, he is a very good writer himself. I thank both of them for all they have done.

Members of Redeemer Lutheran Church—They have always been very positive about my work. Many have encouraged me to continue writing articles for the church newsletter, which I have been doing for the last couple of decades. They let me know how much they liked the Christmas stories I wrote and led me to think about writing this book with just Christmas stories included.

The staff at Northwestern Publishing House— They worked with me to edit my work, fix problems, correct punctuation, do the layouts, put these stories between two covers, and make this book become a reality. I thank them.

INTRODUCTION

There is a "Christian difference" that makes this book stand out from others written about Christmas. Many books have wonderful stories and pictures telling of the beauty of the Christmas season, family traditions, decorating the Christmas tree, etc. The stories are fuzzy, warm, and meant to make the reader feel good. There is nothing wrong with feeling good or reading these books, but my book is different. It is dedicated to the idea that Christmas should center on Christ. Every story in this collection is about things that have happened to me or people I know. The stories help the reader better understand the implications that the birth of Jesus has for each of us—how he was destined to fulfill the prophecies of the Old Testament and become the Savior of the world.

As a child, I could hardly wait for Christmas. Our family did not have a huge income, but there were always plenty of gifts around the tree, lots of good food, wonderful church services, and Christian love. This book contains many of my favorite Christmas stories from years ago and more. What could be better than authoring a book that helps others love and understand the story of Jesus' birth and see how important it is in their lives? By dying on a Roman cross as an adult, Jesus ultimately paid the price for all the sins each of us has committed or will commit in the future. The wages of sin is death. Jesus paid that price, not for his sins but for ours. He defeated the grave, making it possible for those who believe in him to have eternal life in heaven. I pray these stories help remind the reader that Jesus is as real and alive today as he was when he was born in Bethlehem some two thousand years ago.

I can remember heading home from the snow-covered Cascade Mountains, driving my GMC pickup and camper while pulling a loaded two-horse trailer. The cab was piled high with my hunting gear and rifle. I was tired and half-frozen from going on the last November elk hunt of the year earlier that morning. I did what I often do when I need a pick-me-up. I put on Christmas music—beautiful hymns and carols—and turned up the volume. It never gets better than that! I loved every minute of those rides home. I could hardly wait to put up the tree, decorate the house, and start celebrating the birth of the Christ Child. My wife, Ruth, has always insisted we have to get Thanksgiving finished before we start Christmas, but she has her hands full holding me back.

I pray when you read this collection of my favorite Christmas stories, they will renew your excitement and love toward our Savior Jesus—as they do my own every time I read them. God in human form arrived on this earth, not as a sword-wielding rebel but as a tiny baby lying in a manger. He was destined to become the Savior of the whole world. What a story! What a life! What a difference he has made and continues to make in the world today. It is my prayer that these stories will make a real Christian difference for those who take time to read them.

I wish you a blessed Christmas,
John R. Hardison

ONE

PUT BABY JESUS IN YOUR WAGON

The book of *Guinness World Records* says the world's largest collection of nativity sets is in a museum in Feltre, Italy, and contains (as of March 14, 2009) 1,802 different nativities. Surely Mary and Joseph could not have imagined that the humble scene with themselves, baby Jesus in a manger, some livestock, angels, and several shepherds on Christmas Eve night two thousand years ago would be re-created with thousands and thousands of figurines fashioned by craftspeople and factories throughout the world. Because we are told only a few details of that night, almost every nativity set is slightly different. It boggles my mind to think of how many unique nativity sets there are in the world.

Over the years, my wife, Ruth, and I have acquired a variety of nativity sets. We are nowhere near the world record. And many of our sets are, perhaps, too beat up for a museum.

Of course, we have the set that was made by my grandfather and grandmother, which is my favorite.

It consists of the wooden stable, two camels, a couple of sheep, a cow, a donkey, a couple of shepherds, an angel, the three Magi, Mary, Joseph, and the babe in the manger. It fits beautifully on the waist-high top of the cupboard where our good dishes are kept in our dining room. It is my pride and joy as far as Christmas decorations are concerned.

To my wife and me, it is not the price that makes a nativity set valuable but whether it is beautiful, unusual, or interesting. I bought one small set at a yard sale for only a few cents, and it sits on our refrigerator all year round. It is from Alaska. The barn is made like a log cabin, and it has just Mary, Joseph, and the baby Jesus. We like it because it is rather rustic.

We bought one small set while on a trip in Lake City, Colorado. It was made in Israel from olive wood. There were a number of these sets on the store shelf, but each one was slightly different. Ours has circular rings on the piece of olive wood that give the illusion of a cave behind Mary, Joseph, and the baby, which is what some say the actual birthplace may have been.

We have an all-white set made out of a chalklike material. The individual figures of sheep, angels, the child in the manger, and more, are rather small and delicate. Several have been broken and patched. However, this set was given to Ruth by a favorite aunt, so we consider it a keepsake.

We have a very nice-looking set with Mary, Joseph, and the baby Jesus that is supposed to look like it was carved from a single piece of log, though it is actually plastic.

Another set has only Mary, Joseph, and Jesus left because the other pieces were broken when the box was dropped. We love its look and the main pieces are still there, so we continue to use it anyway.

A cross in our dining room pictures various Bible Christmas scenes, making it a very unusual way of showing the nativity.

Ruth even bought a set that is missing Joseph and has only Mary and the Christ Child. People still comment on how beautiful that set is. They never seem to miss the other figures.

My sister rescued the old crèche that came from the five-and-dime store when we were kids. The donkey no longer has a head. The cow is missing an ear. The other figures have been worn with scratches and are a little dirty from the sticky hands of the little ones who have held them through the years. The stable is also a little worse for wear. However, the Christ Child is still laid lovingly in the manger each Christmas as my sister puts the set out with her other crèche scenes that are much newer.

It doesn't matter how expensive the nativity set is or how many figures it has, they all have one thing in common. Even all those 1,802 sets in the record-setting Italian museum collection have this one thing too. They all include the baby Jesus. Take him out of any of these sets and what good is it? With an empty manger, the meaning of Christmas is completely lost. The shepherds and angels as well as Mary and Joseph have no reason to be at that stable if the baby Jesus is not there. He alone is what is important.

I once read a story about a woman who saw a poor little girl looking at an inexpensive nativity set. The child's mother wanted to buy the nativity set but could not afford it. The little girl begged to be allowed to have just the baby Jesus to take home. Out of frustration, the mother became angry with the child and made her put the statue of baby Jesus back on the shelf. A woman who had watched all this let the person at the register know that she would buy the nativity set so that the little girl could take home the statue of baby Jesus, which she was still admiring. The woman took the statue to the register and convinced the mother it would be okay for the child to have it. Each Christmas after that she kept the rest of the nativity set sitting on her desk at work. She told others who asked why there was no statue of the baby that it reminded her of the importance of Jesus in her life and that she felt it was the most important nativity set she owned. I firmly believe she was right.

When Isaiah said, "He will be called Wonderful Counselor, Mighty God, Everlasting Father, Prince of Peace" (Isaiah 9:6) and Luke said, "Today in the town of David a Savior has been born to you; he is the Messiah, the Lord" (Luke 2:11), they were not talking about Mary or Joseph or an angel or any of the other figures in the nativity scenes. They were speaking of Jesus alone.

Maybe you have seen the Christmas episode of the TV show *Dragnet* from many years ago where Sgt. Joe Friday and his partner were called to find a statue of baby Jesus that had been stolen from the nativity scene at a church in a poor neighborhood. Like all the stories on *Dragnet*, this one came from actual police files. Jack Webb, the star and producer of the show, liked this true story so much that in the early 1950s he did an episode on it on both TV and radio in the same week, and then in 1967 he produced another TV version of it, with many of the same actors and almost the same script. I first heard this program on the radio. Later, I saw it on television as well, and I loved it. It was repeated on TV for several years and is now available on DVD, no doubt because people besides myself loved it as well.

When Sergeant Friday and his partner, Frank, get to the church, he describes the nativity set as having one shepherd minus an arm, one sheep with many cracks in it, and, of course, the infant Jesus missing.

That description fits some of our nativity sets, except this one was missing the key piece.

As Sergeant Friday is getting "just the facts," he has an interesting bit of dialogue with the priest. He asks when the church is locked for the night. The priest replies that it stays open all night. Friday is surprised, partly because this is a low-income area of Los Angeles.

"You leave it wide open so any thief can walk in?"

"Particularly thieves, Sergeant," says the priest with a little grin.

I always loved that line. Christmas Eve is especially for thieves and all lost sinners, isn't it? Those are exactly the ones our Savior came to save.

Friday and his partner track down their only suspect. He has a criminal record and was seen leaving the church with a bundle in his arms the size of the Jesus figurine. But the bundle turns out to be just a pair of trousers that someone had mended for him. The two officers reluctantly return to the church to tell the priest they are out of leads and won't be able to find baby Jesus before Christmas Mass.

As the two officers are talking with the priest, the church doors open. Up the long church aisle walks pint-sized Paco Mendoza, pulling his red wagon noisily across the stone floor. When he finally gets close enough, the priest and the two officers see that the Jesus figurine is in his wagon.

Sergeant Friday has the priest ask Paco some questions in Spanish. Finally, the priest explains what happened. Through the years, Paco had been praying for a red wagon. This year, he prayed to the child Jesus and made a promise that if he got the wagon, the child Jesus would have the first ride in it.

By now Paco is in tears. He thinks he is in big trouble. He asks the priest if the devil is going to come and take him down into hell to punish him. So the priest says to little Paco, "No el Diablo. Jesus ama a Paquito mucho." Jesus loves Paquito (little Paco) a lot.

As Paco is leaving with his empty red wagon, the priest tells Sergeant Friday that Paco's family could not afford to get him a wagon. But each year the firefighters refurbish used toys and give them to poor children in the neighborhood. They gave Paco the wagon he had prayed for, so Paco kept his promise to Jesus. It was not enough for Paco to look at Jesus in the nativity set in front of church. He loved Jesus so much that he kept his promise to him to have the first ride in his new wagon. When the ride was done, what did Jesus do? Through the priest, Paco was told that Jesus loves him very much.

Jack Webb opted to put this show on radio and TV several times. I can understand why. People loved this beautiful story and looked forward to seeing it year after year.

This year when you see a nativity scene in front of a church or at someone's home, or when you bring your favorite set (or sets) out to decorate your home, remember which of the figurines gives every nativity set its meaning. Remember that Jesus is not just a nice baby from long ago. He grew up to fulfill the prophesies about the Suffering Servant. He died to pay the price for our sins, but rose from the grave so that Christians will have eternal life. He sits at his Father's right hand, hearing your every heartbeat and knowing your every thought. As in the story of Paco, his door is wide open all night long "so any thief can walk in" — or any other sinners. Like Paco, talk to him. God answered Paco's prayers with a red wagon from the local firefighters. Tell Jesus your prayers. Particularly, tell him the prayers that have gone unanswered for years. He is preparing his answer as you read this. We do not know how he will answer, but you can be sure he *will* answer because God's Word says so.

Finally, don't leave Jesus there in the nativity set. Put him in your "wagon." Make him a part of your everyday life. Ruth and I discovered a long time ago that life is better with Christ at the center. We look forward to reading our devotions just before bed each night and discussing them. Try it. It is fun and comforting. It isn't just nativity sets that are meaningless without Jesus. Every part of our lives is affected either by Jesus or by his absence. There is no middle ground. However, those who keep Jesus at their side can expect to hear his ministers say, just as Paco was told in the *Dragnet* story, "No devil for you. Jesus loves you very much!" The Bible tells us that same message again and again.

Put baby Jesus in your wagon (your life) this year and every year for the long haul, instead of the short haul by putting his statue and the nativity set back in the storage cabinet till next Christmas. 🌿

> *Ah, dearest Jesus, holy Child,*
> *Prepare a bed, soft, undefiled*
> *Within my heart, made clean and new,*
> *A quiet chamber kept for you.*
>
> FROM A HYMN BY MARTIN LUTHER

TWO

ASKING FOR SNOW

One December some 50 years ago, there were cold winds and freezing temperatures but not one flake of snow. There were Christmas decorations and tinsel as well as packages, bags, and ads for discounts and sales. But the roofs were bare, and the nativity scenes sat on brown lawns. The only snow you could find was the artificial snow in the storefront windows, but the crowds of last-minute shoppers didn't stop to notice it. Everyone still said, "Merry Christmas," and no one missed having to shovel. Snowless Christmases in Yakima aren't all that rare. But one little boy, about two-and-a-half years old, had his heart set on seeing snow.

He was eager for Christmas to finally arrive. He was still too young to be in the Sunday school Christmas Eve service, but he was old enough to start having some favorite Christmas hymns and to learn some of the words. He particularly liked "Away in a Manger," "Silent Night," "O Little Town of Bethlehem," and others.

He was proud to be able to buy his mom and dad presents, and his folks had taken him into town to shop. From his weekly allowance he had saved what, in his eyes, was a small fortune. His folks each had made sure to mention to him, in passing, some small thing in his price range that they "really, really wanted." First, Mom took him on a careful search through the store aisles for a present for Dad. Then Dad led him on a search for Mom's gift. The boy wanted the gifts to be just right. These presents were for the two people he loved the most. Back home, he used wrapping paper with angels on it that reminded him about the angels singing to the shepherds, announcing the birth of the babe in a manger. He also showed his love for his parents in the careful way he placed the gifts under his family's Christmas tree.

He did not know about the packages that had come in the mail from grandparents, aunts, and uncles in a faraway state. His parents kept them hidden till after he was in bed on Christmas Eve. He also didn't know Santa's gifts were already hidden in the house.

Christmas Eve day, his folks helped him "write" a note to Santa. He listed a few things he wanted and told Santa there would be cookies and milk waiting for him. Then, toward the end, he asked for one more present: snow on Christmas Day. He signed it with love, put it in an envelope with "To Santa" written on it for him by his mom, and then carefully placed it on the table with the milk and cookies Mom brought out. With the cookies came one more important job: he needed to try a cookie himself, to make sure they tasted okay. Then he was off to bed. Christmas Eve had been busy, and he needed sleep. His parents tucked him in, and he said his prayers. He prayed aloud for his parents, his grandparents, and several special friends. Then, last of all, he asked God to please send some snow, so the world would look more like Christmas. He hoped he and his folks could build a snowman and throw snowballs together.

No snow had been predicted. The weatherman on the black-and-white TV had been anything but hopeful. His mom and dad looked at each other and said a little prayer to themselves that there would be at least a little snow for their only child. Back downstairs, they talked cheerfully as they pulled out the hidden packages and festively wrapped toys. Then they stood back with their arms around each other, checking to be sure all was perfect before heading off to bed.

Up early the next morning, while it was still dark, Mom turned on the coffee maker while Dad lit the tree. They quickly got the fireplace roaring. Dad played Bing Crosby's original Christmas album softly on their old hi-fi. They checked the arrangement of the packages one last time. Mom added a nice "Thank you" from Santa, written carefully on their son's note. They shared the cookies and the milk and had a cup of coffee while the fire took the chill off the room. They looked at each other. Everything was ready.

They climbed noiselessly up the stairs to their son's room. He looked so peaceful that they almost hated to wake him. But after a moment, his mother gently shook him until his eyes began to open. "Santa has been here," she said. Hearing that, the boy's eyes grew wide and he quickly sat up. He headed down the stairs so fast his parents had a hard time keeping up.

The look in his eyes when he saw that beautiful tree with the Christmas star on top and all the packages sitting around it was one his folks would remember always. There was true joy in their eyes as they each opened their special gift from their son. The boy saw that joy and learned from it. Among the boy's many gifts was one large box from his aunt, and as he moved aside the white paper inside the box, he gave a little "Yip" and jumped back with a startled look on his face. He quickly returned and finished moving the paper away from a huge golden teddy bear. He would keep that bear for the rest of his life.

The boy suddenly remembered he had asked for snow. He ran to the front door, asking, "Did it snow? Did it snow?" Mom and Dad braced themselves for the disappointment. The front door was pulled open and the porch light was switched on. The boy saw snow on the ground and more coming down. He jumped up and down for joy. The sudden surprise moved each parent to say a prayer of thanksgiving. In that wonderful moment, all problems were forgotten and the young family truly felt that "peace on earth and good will for men" had arrived.

I love this story from many years ago because the boy who loved the snow was my only son, Gregory Lloyd Hardison. That Christmas when he was about two and a half, we didn't know that God would call our little boy home at age 13. Only God knew. I cannot answer the question *why*. I do know that Greg is now in heaven with Jesus, who has given him peace that will last much longer than the snow he wanted for Christmas. It is my sure hope that one day we will be together again in heaven.

> *"Have you entered the storehouses of the snow*
> *or seen the storehouses of the hail,*
> *which I reserve for times of trouble...?"*
>
> JOB 38:22,23

THREE

BABE'S MANGER

My wife, Ruth; her three sisters; and her baby brother grew up outside the small town of Omak, Washington. Her father, Paul, worked long hours in the local lumber mill. Her mother, Hilda, worked in the local laundry. Money was tight from one pay period to the next.

The family lived on a 5-acre plot 3 miles out of town by way of a steep, winding road. When the last steep grade got icy and slick, the county put out boxes of sand for shoveling onto the icy spots. If sand and car chains failed, all but the driver and the baby would get out and push the car over the last 100 or 200 feet of the grade. Atop that last grade, about half a mile of flat road led to their home.

The Friebus home had been a run-down, two-bedroom house when they originally moved into it. Paul and Hilda worked hard over several years to make it more livable. Paul, a good carpenter, put in many long hours. When they tore down buildings on the property, Ruth's Uncle Arno and her dad used the old lumber to build a new garage and the barn that housed their two milk cows: a Holstein named Rosie and a Guernsey named Babe. They made a small amount of money selling milk and cream as well as eggs, and garden vegetables when they were in season.

On Christmas Eve 1950, the Friebus family piled into their 1939 two-door Plymouth to head to church for the Christmas Eve service. The program went well. Ruth's oldest sister played the pump organ. All three older sisters said their recitations. The service ended with "Silent Night." Each child got a brown paper bag containing hard candy and an orange, a very special treat in those days. Everyone said their "Merry Christmases" to one another, pulled on their heavy coats, and headed out into the cold.

Colored lights brightened the snow-covered streets of Omak. Other people had sanded down the road, so the Friebus' car had no trouble climbing the steep hill home — no pushing the old Plymouth in the cold.

The children were told to wait in the car with their dad while Mom went in "to see if Santa had brought any packages." She lit the Christmas tree lights and set out cookies on plates. Then she brought out all the Christmas gifts from their hiding places and put them around the tree.

Heading back outside toward the car, a thought occurred to Hilda. Babe was due to calve any day. She decided to check the barn on the off chance that Babe had had her calf while the family was at church. A calf's birth was a big deal. The kids had fun watching a new calf's antics. The adults, of course, saw in a new calf the possibility of some extra milk money or an animal they could later butcher for meat. The children were surprised as their mother walked past the car in the garage and headed for the barn. She switched on the one light over the birthing area. There was Babe and not one, but two newborn calves—twins—lying on the straw! The children were called to come and see the special gift God had provided while they had been at church. They were very excited to see the small brown calves. They were a special gift indeed.

Sleep would be long in coming that night due to all the excitement. However, there would be special prayers of thanks for all the gifts, including the special gifts fittingly born on Christmas Eve to Babe near a manger. The calves were a special reminder of that other manger, without even one light over it: the manger that held the baby Jesus.

The Christ Child's birth is so much more special than Babe's twin calves: not just cute and not just bringing a little more milk money, but bringing us salvation.

Ye shall find the babe wrapped in swaddling clothes, lying in a manger.

LUKE 2:12, KJV

FOUR

THE GIFT

For many of us, buying Christmas gifts is a very special part of a special season. We enjoy the challenge of finding just the right gift for each individual on our list—the thrill of finding something that fits each recipient's personality. Like the hunter who has just bagged a trophy buck, we bask in the sense of accomplishment when we finally hunt down the items our loved ones really want. We imagine how their eyes will light up with joy and happiness as they open the gifts.

It reminds me of something that happened at a church Christmas party several years ago. Each person brought some goodies to share and a gift to put under the tree. For the gift exchange, we all drew numbers. Whoever drew the number 1 got first choice of all the gifts under the tree. However, if the person who held number 2 liked the gift the first person had opened, he or she could exchange an unopened gift for that one. The obvious catch was that someone down the line might take the same gift away. This process would continue until all the gifts were claimed.

The evening unfolded into a pleasing display of good fellowship and fun. When it came time for the gift exchange, we were curious not only to see what we would get but to see who would get the gifts we had put under the tree. I think my contribution was a Gene Autry Christmas tape I knew someone would be sure to enjoy. Ruth gave a little handmade angel ornament that would be a beautiful addition to someone's Christmas tree. The exchange was punctuated by peals of laughter and howls of consternation whenever someone would help themselves to a gift someone else had already picked.

Ruth and I were both pleased when our pastor's wife picked up Ruth's brightly wrapped contribution. Colleen is a very gracious person. A little shy, she is an extremely sensitive individual who always puts the best construction on everything. After she carefully unwrapped the box, she looked inside. A hush settled over the group as everyone waited to see what the box contained. However, instead of immediately producing the gift and thus getting out of the limelight, she hesitated. We could all see by the look on her face that she was puzzled and a bit embarrassed. Then she held the box upside down and shook it. Nothing came out. Nothing at all. Searching for the person who gave the box, her eyes scanned the faces around the room.

About then, my mouth dropped open. I was truly speechless! I thought seriously of taking an extended bathroom break. Ruth turned bright red. She took the box from Colleen and looked inside and shook it herself. Talk about a pregnant pause. Ruth finally recovered her senses enough and explained that she must have wrapped the wrong box because there was supposed to be a gift inside. "It was an angel," she stammered, "a sugar-starched, white, crocheted angel. Really!"

Suddenly, absolute silence gave way to uproarious laughter. Colleen's expression had been priceless, as had mine and especially Ruth's. For the rest of the evening, the whole group got a lot of mileage out of this mistake.

But something striking — somewhat odd, yet profound — resulted from this incident. As the exchange continued, the most popular gift, among a lot of very nice ones, was the empty box. Though the box had been there all along, no one had paid much attention to it until they knew it was empty. Then everyone took notice. Everyone wanted it. One after another, people traded for this gift. The most humble gift in the room, an empty box, became the most valued gift because people believed they would ultimately receive something wonderful. Though they didn't really know what that gift would look like, only that it was a crocheted angel, they wanted it because they believed it was worth having!

The Christmas story is like that. When we get through all the trappings of the Christmas season — all the glitter and expensive presents — we see that the most humble present is the most valuable of all. A child was born in as humble a setting as anyone could imagine, wrapped in strips of cloth, and placed in a manger. That child was not much to look at on the surface, and yet he possessed the gift of salvation for us and for the world. Do we understand the full value of this gift? Probably not. Is there some sense of mystery about it? Certainly! But the prophets of Scripture tell us that the gift this humble child brought to the world is the greatest gift we will ever receive: "To us a child is born, to us a son is given, and the government will be on his shoulders. And he will be called Wonderful Counselor, Mighty God, Everlasting Father, Prince of Peace" (Isaiah 9:6).

That's the mystery and meaning of Christmas. God became one of us in order to bring us peace. At the very heart of the Christmas story, sometimes buried deep beneath all the hoopla of the season, is the gift that makes an individual's eyes light up with joy and happiness as no other gift can.

The challenge for you and me during the Christmas season is to extend this great gift to those we know and love. That may not seem to be the fanciest gift, the most expensive gift, or the largest gift. But it is by far the best.

*"What no eye has seen, what no ear has heard,
and what no human mind has conceived"* —
the things God has prepared for those who love him —
these are the things God has revealed to us by his Spirit.

1 CORINTHIANS 2:9,10

FIVE

CHRISTMAS EVE AT THE HOSPITAL

Friday, December 21, 2012, had been a long day. Ruth and I had been out shopping, getting ready for Christmas. Dinner was finished and the dishes were washed. About 8:30 we were sitting in our easy chairs watching some Christmas programs on TV. Ruth was trying her best to write out a few last-minute Christmas cards while she watched. Hilda, my mother-in-law, was watching TV in the kitchen. Everything seemed as normal as decorating the house for Christmas in December.

As I half-dozed in my chair, Ruth said, "I think I'll go lie down for awhile." I said fine as she went downstairs to take a nap—or so I thought. About 45 minutes later, the phone rang. "Who could be calling?" I thought to myself. I put the phone to my ear—it was Ruth! "I'm sick," she said. "I'm on the floor of the basement spare bedroom and too weak to get up." It was all she could do to call me on her cell phone.

I hurried downstairs. Ruth was sick to her stomach and very weak. I hollered to Hilda to come downstairs. After a short discussion with her, I called an ambulance. Our neighbor who is a fireman arrived first and helped the ambulance find us. We live a ways off the road, and it was a snowy winter night.

It was an 8-mile ambulance ride to Memorial Hospital, and by the time Ruth arrived, she was throwing up and had developed diarrhea. I thought she had a bad case of the flu. On the CAT scans, her colon looked inflamed. Finally, at 3 A.M. Saturday morning, she was admitted.

When I returned to the hospital late Saturday morning, she was about the same, except the nausea was being controlled. The doctors had ordered blood tests but still did not know what was wrong with her. I spent several hours with Ruth and then went home to check on Hilda. I came back to the hospital later, but they still did not know anything new and were not ready to send her home. I told Ruth I loved her and would see her after church the next day. It didn't seem there was anything going on that was of great concern.

On Sunday Hilda did not feel like going to church, so I went alone. I asked Pastor Schwartz to include a prayer for Ruth in church and did a lot of praying for her myself. I missed having her there at church with me. I can get pretty emotional, and Ruth and I have always been quite close. I have no idea what the sermon that morning was about, but I know I prayed a lot. I felt church was the natural place to be, and people were very supportive. Many went out of their way to tell me they were praying for Ruth. After Bible study I went to lunch with the usual group from church, including my friend Gail and his wife. Then I went to see what the doctors were doing about Ruth and her tests. There was still no information, and there still seemed to be little concern. I expected them to send her home that afternoon. I told Ruth she could call me on my cell if she was ready to go home. We both had past experiences with being released from hospitals and understood that it generally took all day. I went home in the evening, and Hilda and I figured out something for supper. I called Ruth to say goodnight and to tell her I loved her. She told me she loved me, and we hung up the phone. I said my prayers, read a devotion, and went to bed thinking everything was going to be fine.

When I finally got to sleep, I slept hard as my body caught up on the missed sleep from the two previous nights. The phone rang at 8 A.M., but I did not hear it. Hilda answered it and then worked her way down the stairs while yelling for me to wake up: the hospital people needed to talk to me! Through a sleepy haze I heard the nurse tell me Ruth's blood pressure had dropped extremely low. They were giving her blood transfusions, but the nurse said I had better get there quickly. Suddenly, I was fully awake. I drove those 8 miles as quickly as I could.

Later I found out that around 3 A.M. Ruth had called the nurse to help her to the bathroom. As she stood up, she fainted in the nurse's arms. The nurse hit the intercom button and called for emergency help. They knew something was really wrong and discovered at that point that she was losing a lot of blood. However, Ruth, although almost out cold, made them wait until 8 A.M. to call me. She later told me she had wanted me to get more sleep.

Reaching Ruth's room, I saw how pale she was. She was barely conscious. The nurses' concerned expressions told me, without them having to say it directly, that they had almost lost her and still might. They were administering the third pint of blood as fast as possible through her IV. They said the internist and the surgeon were on the way. I prayed they would hurry. It seemed like forever before the surgeon arrived. New CAT scans showed Ruth was bleeding in or around her colon. The surgeon said he had no choice but to do exploratory surgery, try to locate exactly where she was bleeding, and fix the problem. I remember telling him to do what needed to be done. He said he'd do his very best and then was gone. Before I could get to the surgery floor and the waiting room, Ruth had already been taken into surgery.

I prayed a lot more: "God, your will be done. But, if possible, let Ruth be okay!"

It was December 24. At home, the music Ruth and I were supposed to sing with the choir at church that evening sat in a stack. Only some of our packages had been wrapped. And only some of those had been put under the tree. All our Christmas plans had been abruptly canceled.

I called Hilda and told her what I knew. I had previously called my sister and brother. Ruth's name was now on prayer chains in Washington, California, Missouri, and Montana. I phoned two friends, Gail Thornton and Don Butler, who came to the hospital and kept me company. That sure helped. Minutes slowly ticked by. Liz, another friend, came by and asked me if I had eaten. I had not even thought about eating. The burger she went and got sure tasted good. One hour, then two went by. The surgeon had said it would take about two hours. I prayed, talked, and prayed some more.

At last, after a little more than three hours, the surgeon came out to talk to me. He looked solemn and did not say anything. It flashed across my mind that he had lost her. When he finally spoke, he said she would be fine. Part of the large intestine had been in such bad shape that he had to cut out 18 inches of it and stitch the rest of the intestine back together. Since the large intestine is about 5-feet long, he said she would fully recover in a couple of months and never miss those 18 inches. I managed to thank him before the lump in my throat got too big and the tears began to run down my face.

Although God wasn't telling any of us, he had this all figured out ahead of time. If the bleeding had begun while she was at home, she could have died. If they had not kept her in the hospital, she probably would have died. And no one has been able to explain to us why she had the flu-like symptoms that caused her to be taken to the hospital in the first place.

It was time for prayers of thanksgiving. Thanks that my prayers and those of the many prayer-chain people had been answered. Thanks that God was in control. Thanks for those unexplained flu symptoms. Thanks that the rest of the church choir sang well without us. As Christmas Eve turned to Christmas Day, all seemed right with the world. Ruth and I knew very well we had been the beneficiaries of a wonderful Christmas miracle. I knew I had received a very special Christmas gift I would not soon forget.

Always remember we are blessed to have our loved ones kept safe by our dear Lord Jesus' guiding hand.

Ruth and I wish you and yours a blessed, Christ-filled Christmas!

We need you, O Lord Jesus,
To be our dearest friend.
Your love will guard and guide us
And keep us to life's end.
Your love will guard and guide us
And keep us to life's end.

FROM THE HYMN, "WHEN CHRISTMAS MORN IS DAWNING,"
© 1978 *LUTHERAN BOOK OF WORSHIP;* ADMIN. AUGSBURG
FORTRESS. ALL RIGHTS RESERVED. USED WITH PERMISSION.

SIX

SING-ALONGS WITH CLARA AND MOLLY

When Ruth and I were first married, we invited a few friends over each year for Christmas sing-alongs. The group grew until we were hosting 30 or more people each Christmas. In 1995 we started inviting people from church as well for a night of fun, food, fellowship, and singing.

Ruth had put together a songbook, which she used with her elementary school students when she took them to sing carols at a local nursing home. Over the years we retyped every page in that songbook several times, adding new verses and songs, but we still use the original covers, hand-colored by Ruth's fourth graders.

We decorate our house from top to bottom. Downstairs, where we hold the sing-along, we put up a western tree. All the decorations are cowboy items. There are plenty of colored lights, a burning fire, pictures with Christmas themes, and, of course, Gene Autry Christmas albums. We enjoy silly games, laughter, Christian fellowship, and the wonderful singing of our friends. These make all the preparations worthwhile. What better way to celebrate the birth of our Lord than to praise him with Christian fun and songs?

Everybody joins in to make a joyful noise. We make mistakes and have a good laugh. Since 1996, I have recorded our singing each year. One of the things that give Ruth and I the most pleasure each Christmas season is listening to these CDs. They never fail to bring some smiles. Each year's Christmas sing-along has a character of its own and usually a few new hams as well. Fun, camaraderie, and love of the Lord are evident on each recording. Some songs repeat from year to year, but they are never sung exactly the same way. In addition, each year we learn a new song or two, singing them with joy and gusto.

In the fall of 1998, I wrote one of those new songs myself. I was helping my friend Gail round up cattle from his 45,000-acre range high in the Cascade Mountains. It generally takes more than 30 days of hard riding to gather all the cattle. These mountains are steep and covered with rockslides, brush, and timber.

We had located a bunch of the cattle and were herding them toward the holding pasture and corrals south of Rimrock Lake. Among them was a white cow along with her calf—the only white cow Gail had in his herd. As we approached the holding pasture, the trail passed through some thick timber and brush. We kept whooping and hollering, guiding the cattle toward the entrance. Things were going well, or so we thought, until we discovered we had gotten all the cattle into the corrals except that one white cow.

I asked what the story was on the white cow. Gail said his friend's grandson had named her Clara. She didn't like to be caught and had a bad habit of turning off the trail into the thick brush and hiding while the rest of the cows and the riders went by.

We backtracked half a mile and made another push, checking all the brushy areas. We found Clara and her calf and got them started once more toward the entrance to the pasture. One of the other riders, named Robbie, stayed right with her through brush and timber and made sure she went into the pasture. With lots of whistles and hollering, Robbie pushed her through the entrance to the pasture and headed for the corral. But he pushed her through the open corral gate on the run. In fact, he pushed her so fast she went into the corral and promptly jumped the fence on the opposite side and started up the hillside! Gail saw what was happening. Galloping his horse through the corral, he opened the gate near where she had jumped the fence and rode after her. He chased her for a mile over some of the roughest terrain in the Cascades but couldn't catch her.

Gail told me later, she had been hard to catch and had gotten away from several people in the past. She liked to stay in the high country as long as possible and was almost always the very last cow to be rounded up. She was meek as a kitten when trucked home, and she produced great calves, but she often wasn't home till nearly Christmas.

Later that fall, I told Ruth I was going to write lyrics to a song about Clara, which could be sung to the tune of "Here Comes Santa Claus." The first verse went like this:

Here comes Clara Cow! There goes Clara Cow!
Right down Rimrock Lane.
Gail and Dona and all the riders
Are chasing her in vain.
Gail is "Whooping," cowboys yelling,
All is running in fright!
Count your blessings and say your prayers
'Cause Clara's not home tonight!

Gail and Dona are regulars at our sing-alongs. The first time we sang that song, Gail turned as red as Santa's suit and everyone had a lot of laughs. It became an annual sing-along standard.

Then came the summer of 2003: hot and dry and extreme danger of forest fires. No open campfires were allowed. Even the logging camps were shut down for a few weeks. On one of the worst days of the heat wave, I happened to look from our patio at the mountains to the northwest. I noticed a cloud of smoke and was immediately concerned about the cattle I knew Gail had up there in their summer range. I called Gail, and he said he needed men and horses right away to help get those cattle down Cowiche Canyon to his home ranch. I loaded my horse and pulled into his driveway an hour later. A number of men, horses, trucks, and trailers were there already. I backed my horse out of my trailer and loaded him into Gail's larger trailer. Then everyone headed up Cowiche Canyon toward the fire. About 12 miles up we stopped the rigs, unloaded, and saddled the horses. Then we split up to hunt for those cattle.

We knew if the wind shifted and became stronger the fire could quickly move down the canyon and destroy much of Gail's herd, along with many cabins and homes that were already being evacuated. We needed to get his cattle down the canyon and out of danger as soon as possible. It took all day, but we managed to get the vast majority out. Some were still missing, but Gail's range contained thousands of acres. We couldn't have found them all in just one day.

As it turned out, the wind did not send the fire down Cowiche Canyon after all. No homes or cabins were burnt. No cows were lost. Even those the riders had missed came down safely over the next few weeks. A month later, one of the very last missing cows and her calf made their way to the lower elevations and finally joined the rest of the herd. Gail's grandson Brandon had named her Molly. She was Gail's only white cow, since Gail had sold Clara a couple years earlier. It seemed she was going to take Clara's place in more ways than one.

When our Christmas sing-along came around that December, Molly's story was told. The party group heard about the fire and how Molly was one of the very last to come down. Remembering the stories of Clara, they began to chuckle.

I also told the group how Molly, along with half of Gail's herd, had finally been trucked to his range 35 miles east of his home ranch. This was to be their winter range. In late November it had snowed a couple of inches, and most of the ridge where Gail's cattle were wintered still had snow. I told how, after that snowstorm, Gail and I had taken some cows to market in the lower valley. On our way home he said he wanted to check his cattle on the south side of the ridge. So we drove east till we could see the hillside with his cows. He looked and looked for some time. I asked him what he was trying to find. After a lot of hesitation, he finally said, "A white cow." That made the sing-along group roar with laughter.

It turns out, Gail had not seen Molly since he had turned her out on that range. We could not find her on the south side, so we drove 30 miles around to the north side of the ridge. Molly was not in sight! Leo, a loyal member of our sing-along group, pointed out that, of course, it was probably hard to see a white cow in the snow. As that comment soaked in, there was renewed laughter. The group loved the story so far.

I told them Gail had gone back the next day and had skidded his way up to the very top of the ridge. At that point of the story, Gail broke in: "I found her! I could finally sleep at night! I hadn't seen her since she had been turned out." The group laughed even more.

Then Gail told the group, "I am not letting any grandkids name anymore cows!" Everyone roared once more.

This seemed to be a good time to sing "Here Comes Clara Cow." But toward the end of the song Leo began substituting "Molly Cow" for "Clara Cow." The whole group picked it up and sang "Molly" in place of "Clara." Gail didn't mind at all. If he can turn one of his problems into something that makes others laugh, he will, and he'll laugh right along with them.

I don't know of many other people who have sing-alongs like ours. Maybe sing-alongs in general are a thing of the past. Maybe you have the musical ability and a big enough house to host a sing-along yourself. Do not forget to invite some people who might be interested in learning more about the true meaning of the Christ Child's story but aren't members of a church. Raising a joyful noise to the Lord in this way during the Christmas season is a real blessing for all who participate. You will create memories and cement friendships that will last a lifetime.

If you decide you want to start a sing-along, always reach out to those who have strayed like Gail's two cows Clara and Molly. Some people are like those strays in that they seem to have something holding them back from becoming involved in their church. Ruth and I have found that a personal invitation to our sing-along—a simple phone call letting them know they are wanted—often helps bring them back into the fold. Ask them to come for good food, singing, and joyful, warm Christian hospitality. It might be just what they need to help the Holy Spirit round them up, so to speak, and get them off that ridge filled with sinful danger before the wind shifts and they are lost, as Gail's cattle might have been. Wind can shift very quickly, so do not delay. If you cannot host a sing-along, find another activity where you call and personally invite people to fellowship with other Christians at Christmastime. Be creative. Do it this year.

That is the kind of roundup the best Christmas carols tell us about, isn't it? After all, it was because we had all gone astray that God's own Son arrived as a newborn, was tempted by the devil, spoke of love, died for our sins, and rose from the grave. His love for our souls is such that he won't be satisfied until the last stray turns up. Think what a sing-along there will be when he finally gets us into the corral! Let us practice for it now.

Blessed are those who have learned to acclaim you. . . .
They rejoice in your name all day long.

PSALM 89:15,16

SEVEN

A LESSON FROM A USED CHRISTMAS TREE

The phone rang.

It was near Christmastime. We had decorated two trees, one for the upstairs and one for the basement. The tree in the basement was mainly there for the two Christmas gatherings we had that year, one for a group of schoolteachers and friends and one for the members of our church.

Outside it was snowy and cold. The temperatures had been dipping into the single-digit range several nights in a row. The skies were clear, and it seemed as if every star shone more brightly than usual. The fireplace felt particularly good as Ruth and I wrapped a few more packages and placed them under the upstairs tree, while we listened to Christmas records on the stereo.

Everything seemed right. After all, what could be wrong a few days before the celebration of the birth of the Son of God in a manger? What a great time of year to give thanks to God for all the wonderful things he had given us. In particular, it was a time to remember the gospel message and the free gift of salvation through the death and resurrection of our Savior, this humble babe whose birth we were preparing to celebrate.

I picked up the phone on the third ring, wondering who would be calling us that late in the evening. On the other end was the voice of a close friend. He seemed far away. He made small talk for a few minutes. It was unusual for him to call at that time of night, and I wondered what he really wanted or needed.

He had been having some serious medical problems, but since a major operation, he was now doing well. I asked how the family was, and he indicated everyone was fine. Then he asked how our parties had gone. I told him fine. Then he asked me if we would be using the basement tree anymore this year. He knew that after the parties, we spent most of our time upstairs. I told him we were pretty much through with the basement tree and asked, "Why?"

He said he was wondering if his family could use it since they didn't decorate their tree till Christmas Eve. After a little pause while I caught my breath, I said we would be happy to let them have the tree. We would take our stuff off it, and they could pick it up when they liked. They did get the tree that year, and they did use it to the glory of God in their Christian home.

I have thought about that phone call many times. It must have been hard to call and ask for a secondhand tree. What makes it worse for me is that I was too slow to see what was happening before that call was necessary. The medical expenses were too much for the family budget. The family needed help and I, as well as other Christian friends, was too slow to see it before this father was put in that position. We all knew a major operation had been performed. All who called themselves friends of that family should have realized there would be a shortage of money and helped out.

That event happened many years ago, and I still think about how so many Christian people, including myself, missed the opportunity to let the light of the gospel message brought by the babe in the manger shine. When shepherds were out in the field and the angels appeared to them, they didn't fully understand, but they went to see. When they had found all that the angels had told them about, they went out and spread the word about the coming of the Christ Child. They knew all too well mankind's need for a Savior. They were motivated by the angels' message to respond by pointing others to the Savior.

This Christmas season, take time out from the tinsel and shopping. Look especially for opportunities to reach out to those who need help. The Holy Spirit encourages us, as Christians, to share the Good News and to do good works all year round. Let us spread the message brought by the Christ Child and assist those who could use a hand up. We all know someone who needs to hear the gospel or could use a little cheering up, a small gift of encouragement, a little extra cash, or another person to talk with. This is not some rare thing. As you read this, someone near you needs the gospel message and a helping hand.

Let us pray that the Holy Spirit will open our eyes so that we can see those needs and avoid putting anyone in the position of having to ask for a secondhand tree. What better season of the year to follow God's example of giving the very best, which for him was giving his innocent Son to die on a cross for our sins. 🍃

Since you excel in everything—in faith, in speech, in knowledge, in complete earnestness and in the love we have kindled in you—see that you also excel in this grace of giving. For you know the grace of our Lord Jesus Christ, that though he was rich, yet for your sake he became poor, so that you through his poverty might become rich.

2 CORINTHIANS 8:7,9

EIGHT

A SEASON TO REMEMBER

My son, Greg, turned 12 in 1976.

He was looking more grown up with every passing day. He rode his ten-speed bike a lot. He liked to wear jeans, tennis shoes, a blue denim coat, dark glasses, and a floppy hat.

That fall, Greg spent hours working on the fort he was constructing in our backyard. He took every loose panel and board he could find and nailed them together. When he was finally finished, he had built a fort roughly 3-feet tall, 8-feet wide, and 12-feet long, with a roof covering it in case of rain or snow. A burlap sack covered the doorway. He would sometimes take a sleeping bag out and stay overnight, using his flashlight to see inside. He painted some of the panels. He also put up decorations such as signs with wood-burned messages and peace signs painted on the panels. My favorite was a sign he made with "Jesus is the kiy to life" burned into it. Yes, he spelled *key* with an *i*.

As soon as Thanksgiving was over that year, Greg was involved in preparations for the Christmas Eve program at church. Each Sunday afternoon after church and Sunday school, those who were helping with the program would spend several hours with the young people practicing their singing and recitations. Greg enjoyed it, but like most kids, he was apprehensive about getting up in front of the congregation.

One day, the three of us went to the local high school's tennis courts where fresh Christmas trees were being sold to raise money for the band. We picked a tall, rather full Douglas fir. As usual, after we tied it on top of our old Buick and got it home, we had to cut off a rung of branches to get it into the house. When we finally got it securely in the tree stand, it was beautiful and smelled of the western forests. We used the extra branches as decorations around the house, because they looked and smelled so nice. We took our time getting all the Christmas decorations unpacked and placed on the tree. Greg put on a little snowman and snowwoman he had given to Ruth and me. The year before he had given us a Mr. and Mrs. Santa Claus set of decorations. We made sure those were up as well. Ruth and I still put them up each year. He also put on some of the old paper decorations he had put together as a young child. Hanging tinsel on each branch took a long time, but Greg worked right alongside us. By the time we were done, it was dark outside. When we turned on the tree lights, it looked beautiful.

At school Greg was practicing the songs on his trombone that the band would be playing in the school Christmas program. He learned his parts well. On the night of the program, the gym was packed with parents and friends. The kids sang and played a mixture of secular and religious songs. Some religious songs and skits were still allowed in 1976. It was fun to watch Greg play his trombone. He did a nice job, and he loved getting recognition for all the practicing he had done.

Christmas vacation finally arrived. Greg spent half the time with his mother and half with Ruth and me. The three of us went skiing, though none of us skied very well at that time. It was fun to watch Greg shoot down the hill only halfway under control. Turning to Ruth, I commented, "When you are young, there is no fear." Greg took a few lessons and improved as the ski season continued. He truly loved snow skiing. He could not get enough of it.

Ruth and I took turns taking Greg shopping for gifts for each other. He chose things he thought were special for each of us and paid for them out of his allowance. He wrapped them himself. Packages arrived from grandparents, aunts, and uncles. It looked like Santa had spilled his whole sack of gifts under our tree. I still remember the way the tree was reflected in all its glory by the three big windows along the front of our house. The view from outside was outstanding as well. We hated to turn the tree lights off when we left, because it looked so wonderful through those front windows when we returned. However, neighbors had lost their home to a fire, and the thought of the tree catching fire, especially as it got drier, made me turn the lights off if no one was home.

Greg went to church with us Christmas Eve to say his recitation in the church program. It was fun watching him up there dressed in his nicest Sunday clothes. I think he enjoyed it in spite of being a little anxious about doing anything in front of a group of people. The church looked nice that evening with a huge colorful Christmas tree in the front. A crèche set with nativity figures about 6 inches tall was on the altar in the front of the church. It looked very much like the real thing. We all loved the singing. I no longer remember the exact songs, but everyone sang joyously. It was wonderfully uplifting. I do remember that at the end of the program it got very quiet. The service closed with "Silent Night," sung first in German and then in English. It was just right. As we walked out of the church, Greg collected one of the plain brown paper bags with hard candy and various kinds of goodies that were given to everyone under age 14 or so. Pastor gave us a firm handshake, wished us a Merry Christmas, and told Greg that he did a fine job. We mingled with other friends who also wished us a Merry Christmas and the very best for the New Year.

There was hardly any snow on the road as we drove home. Snow had been a little scarce that year in Yakima Valley. There was just enough on the trees and ground to feel like we were having a white Christmas. We opened the packages that night because Greg was going to his mother's house on Christmas morning. Knowing Greg had been so taken with the erector set that I had as a child, we gave him a steam engine kit. We did not have time to really learn to run it that evening, because there were too many other gifts. Greg got some new shirts and some new pants and socks, and even though he smiled when he got them, I knew he was looking for something that was fun. He found that in one of the original Pong video games. Those of you who are old enough may remember sitting in front of the TV with a funny ball going back and forth on the screen, directed by the two controls sticking up from the Telstar play station. It had sound effects that sounded like a regular Ping-Pong game. After a few days, the sound from that game just about drove us mad. We finally told Greg he had to turn the volume way down. Greg loved playing that game. He wanted us to play over and over again, which we tried, for a while, to accommodate.

The day after Christmas, Greg made the 200-mile journey with us to Ruth's mom and dad's home in Omak, Washington. It was a nice drive. As we got farther north, the snow on the hills along the way made it seem more like Christmas.

We had encouraged Greg to take his steam engine with him and let Paul Sr. (Ruth's dad) help him get it going. Paul was in the process of building a huge metal scale model of a steam tractor. He had started it from a kit and had been working on it for years. He finally did get it so it would run on compressed air, but that was a couple of years in the future. Paul took Greg down to his workshop and spent quite awhile showing him all about how he had put it together so far. He told how each little part worked and how, one day, he would have it up and running. Greg loved every minute of it. He and Greg spent hours working with Greg's new steam engine and learning how to make it go fast.

We got back to Yakima in time to do two things that were important to Greg. One was to attach the Pong game to the TV, which, by the way, only got four channels using an aerial at that time. Once the game was hooked up, it was on a good part of each day, although Greg was good about doing his homework first. The second important thing was to attend church and see his friends. Greg loved to go to church and Sunday school. He believed Christ had been born for all of us and especially for him.

For Ruth and me, that was a wonderful Christmas season to remember: our last Christmas with Greg before he died in an accident the following July. He was a loving, easygoing, responsible child. After the previous couple of years when there had been deaths in the family and my divorce, so many things were going right. I do not know why God chose to take Greg to live in his heavenly home. Ruth and I believe that "in all things God works for the good of those who love him, who have been called according to his purpose" (Romans 8:28). Do those of us who knew and loved Greg miss him? Yes. I wish Greg was here each year when we decorate the tree, attend the Christmas programs at church, watch those wonderful old home movies of Greg as a child, sit through *A Christmas Carol* one more time, and do a hundred and one other things, but he is not. He is in a far better place. Perhaps there are forts, steam engines, Pong games, and ski hills in heaven. Whatever else those in heaven have, they have the perfect joy of seeing their Savior face to face. That's where Greg is, because, as the sign on his fort said for all the neighborhood to see, he knew that "Jesus is the kiy to life."

This Christmas, make sure your loved ones know that "kiy" too. We only have so many Christmases. 🌿

*Teach us to number our days,
that we may gain a heart of wisdom.*

PSALM 90:12

Ruth and I during one of our Christmas sing-alongs

Greg and his teddy bear

The rifle Gramp gave me in 1954

Greg and his dog, Wimpy, ready to hit the road

Two of our many crèche sets

Greg and I look at his new steam engine

Two of our nephews enjoy sugar cookies

Another of our crèche sets

Greg and his Christmas snow

My mother-in-law Hilda's church

Interior of my mother-in-law's church in Stuttgart, Kansas

The stable Gramp made for me

NINE

BLACK ICE

My good friend Gail Thornton said I could include this one. He has a way of telling a story. At the time this story took place, he was a student in the first seventh-grade class I ever taught. A pleasant, quiet young man, Gail went on to become one of the most successful ranchers in Yakima County and the 2006 Yakima County Cattleman's Association Rancher of the Year. Gail has served as president of Redeemer Evangelical Lutheran Church as well as in other church council positions. This is adapted from an article he wrote for Redeemer's newsletter in December 2008.

On the morning of December 24, 1964, our mother and her five children, ages 9 months to 13 years, piled into our old Plymouth. The car was packed with suitcases and Christmas gifts in anticipation of spending the holidays with grandparents, aunts, uncles, and cousins in Springfield, Oregon, some 300 miles from our Yakima home. Excitement was high as Mom drove us out of town.

Less than halfway there, our hopes of a Christmas in Springfield were dashed when, shortly after crossing the summit of Satus Pass, my mother hit a strip of black ice, lost control of the vehicle, slid off the road, and crashed into a ditch filled with rocks. The car's front end was bent to the point it was no longer drivable, but thanks be to God, none of us were physically harmed. A short time later, a state patrol officer appeared and called a wrecker, who towed us to a repair shop north of Goldendale, Washington.

Being the oldest, I could see the fear and uncertainty showing through the tears in my mother's eyes. I could not keep from thinking about the fact that earlier in the year my mom and dad had been divorced. She was doing her best on a very limited income to make Christmas special for us five kids. My mother was a very hardworking, devoted Christian who made Redeemer Church and Jesus focal points of our young lives.

Our family spent the rest of the daylight hours in the waiting room of the repair shop waiting for our car to be made drivable. The mechanics warned us to return to Yakima and not risk driving the damaged car any farther away from home without further repairs. We were tired and mentally drained by the time my mom had driven the 70 miles back to Yakima. Our prayers were answered when we safely reached the outskirts of town.

Redeemer's Christmas Eve service was over by the time we arrived back in Yakima. We went straight over to our Aunt Corky's house. Being around our Christian family members, it was soon feeling like Christmas again.

Looking back, I know what it was that turned the Christmas of 1964 from a disappointment to a fine celebration. While I don't remember any of the gifts under the tree, I do remember the love and support of a Christian mother, fellow family members, Christian friends, and a loving God. That year ended up being one of our most memorable and blessed Christmases ever.

Our lives and situations may change from one Christmas to the next, or even in the course of a single Christmas Eve day, but the love of a forgiving God remains constant, offering us peace and certainty in a world where there otherwise seems to be none. God's Word tells us that "neither death nor life, neither angels nor demons, neither the present nor the future, nor any powers, neither height nor depth, nor anything else in all creation, will be able to separate us from the love of God that is in Christ Jesus our Lord" (Romans 8:38,39).

Where do we find that unchangeable love? The Romans 8 verse says, "in Christ Jesus our Lord"—in the baby who came at Christmas, the baby who grew up and made this promise the night before he died for our sins: "Peace I leave with you; my peace I give you. I do not give to you as the world gives" (John 14:27).

Jesus Christ is the same yesterday and today and forever.

HEBREWS 13:8

TEN

SUGAR COOKIES

My grandmother Myrtle Hardison was a Christian lady who loved to cook. Her specialty was cookies and pies. I can still close my eyes and smell the sweet aroma of her cooking as I walked past my grandparents' house on my way home from the school bus stop. Of course, sometimes I would have to stop in and check to be sure the cookies were coming out okay. She always brought out a plate of cookies and a glass of milk. One of my many favorites was her sugar cookies that she would make at Christmastime. Here is the recipe.

3 cups flour
1 teaspoon baking powder
¼ teaspoon salt
1¼ cups sugar
1 cup Crisco or butter
3 eggs
1 teaspoon lemon or vanilla

Sift dry ingredients. Add shortening and mix. Add eggs and flavoring. Roll very thin on floured board. Cut with floured cutters. Bake at 375 degrees for 8 minutes and decorate.

ELEVEN

BEHIND THE DOOR

When Dad bagged his first deer of the hunting season in the fall of 1954, my prayers started in earnest: "God, please give me a rifle of my own."

I had been interested in hunting since Dad first let me tag along on some hunts, and I had read every hunting magazine and book I could find. I had already been shooting small arms for three years under Dad's and Granddad's supervision. Dad was very proud of his deer that fall and told a lot of people about it. I was proud of him too. The more people Dad told, the more I wanted my own deer rifle so I could be like him.

And every night I prayed for it.

It never entered my mind, but God was already answering my prayer.

I was the oldest of my generation, and Granddad, or Gramp, as family members lovingly called him, was like a second father to me. When I was a little kid, I sat by his chair and listened to his stories of coyotes, weasels, rabbits, chickens, foxes, mountain lions, and more. He trapped a mountain lion on New Year's Day 1913 and had the mounted skin and head to prove it. He loved to tell that story. He had done a lot of hunting and trapping when he was young, and he loved to tell those stories too.

It was largely Gramp who taught me to shoot, hunt, and love the outdoors. We hunted jackrabbits and squirrels. We had target practice with a variety of rifles and pistols. I sometimes think we kept the local hardware store in business buying ammunition and targets. It was Gramp who hammered home safety rules when handling and firing guns. He loved to shoot and was quite a marksman. I wanted a rifle so I could be like Gramp.

With my parents' blessing and unbeknownst to me, Gramp had started looking for a rifle he could afford to repair on his own and give to me for Christmas.

More than once I told God (and my folks, and Gramp, and anyone who would listen) that it didn't have to be a fancy rifle, just usable.

But Gramp wanted it to be special for me. He talked to his sister, whose husband had owned a lot of rifles before he passed away. From those rifles he picked out a Winchester 30-30 Model 94. It looked like he could fix it up nicely. A 30-30 is a good deer rifle for a young person, because it doesn't have as much recoil as some other guns. As the story went, the gun was also an interesting historical piece because in 1910 a Texas Ranger had carried it around.

Soon something happened to get me praying even more. Dad bagged a second buck. It was even bigger than the first. Two bucks in one year was an outstanding accomplishment, which caused even more hunting stories to circulate. I sure was proud, and I sure was praying, "God, please get Mom and Dad to let me have a rifle of my own."

Two big roadblocks stood in my way. At least that's the way I had it figured. First, rifles were expensive. Mom did not work, so the sole source of income was Dad's salary and money was tight. David and Marion, my younger brother and sister, needed things as well. Second, I believed Mom and Dad felt I was too young to handle a big game rifle safely, even though I had always followed my dad's or granddad's instructions when hunting small game. At least *I* thought I had.

With all that figuring, I'm not sure I was very confident in my prayers.

Meanwhile, behind his workshop doors, Gramp had that 30-30 all taken apart. He was sanding the wooden stock, getting it ready to be refinished. He was cleaning each metal part as well, taking off any rust.

When my extended family gathered at my grandparents' home for Thanksgiving dinner, I didn't think to go check Gramp's workshop. I didn't notice any wood stain or bluing acid on his fingers. But I sure heard a lot of hunting stories. Deer season had been closed only a short time and my dad, two uncles, and Gramp spent a good part of the day reliving every deer they had bagged or seen that year as well as retelling their successful hunts from times past. And of course, my dad retold the story of his two large Pacific blacktail bucks, one four-point (ten-point eastern count) and one three-point (eight-point eastern count), and everyone gave him his proper recognition. I was the oldest of all the grandchildren, and how I wanted to have hunting stories of my own to share, to be accepted into the adult circle of family hunters. But I couldn't have my own Thanksgiving deer hunting stories without my own rifle. More intensely than ever, I prayed every night that my folks would see their way clear to somehow buy me one for Christmas.

God must have smiled at my prayers. He knew Gramp was all but finished refurbishing my rifle behind his workshop doors.

In the days leading up to Christmas, we decorated our house and tree, bought gifts, and sang our favorite carols. During the week before Christmas, my brother, sister, and I helped tell the glorious story of the birth of the Christ Child. That church program was a highlight for me. People crowded the church pews. The large choir's Christmas hymns and the more than 250 voices of the congregation never failed to send chills up my back, and that night was no exception. I knew I had already received the most wonderful Christmas gift I ever could, without question: the salvation of my soul, through God's Son as the child whose birth we were celebrating. My parents and grandparents had impressed this on my mind and heart long before I turned 12 years old. I thanked God for that then, and I thank them even more all these years later.

After the service, when it was dark, our family of five piled into our 1948 Chevrolet and my father drove slowly around the streets of Fillmore, California—my hometown—admiring the beautiful colored lights and symbols that celebrated Jesus' birth and listening to Christmas carols on the AM radio. The whole family enjoyed Gene Autry's *Melody Ranch Theater.* Once a year, Gene told in song and words the story of the nativity, which was heard all over the United States. Finally, as we talked excitedly about what might be under our Christmas tree, Dad drove the 5 miles to our ranch and home.

Then somehow, some way, Christmas morning was upon us. Under the beautiful lighted tree were lots of gifts, colorfully wrapped and arranged with loving care by my folks. Everyone's eyes shone brightly as adults and kids alike took turns opening their gifts. But when the last gift had been opened, there was no rifle for me.

To myself I moaned, "I guess they really don't trust me."

Later in the day we went to my maternal grandparents' home for dinner with our extended family and to exchange a few more gifts. We said grace. The food was delicious. And then we went to the living room to open more packages.

It was clear that none of the packages under the tree were the right size or shape to be a rifle. I wonder now if Gramp and my folks noticed how disappointed I was right then. Each person opened his or her gifts, and soon all but one had been unwrapped. It was a tiny box in colorful wrapping. I can still remember the little twinkle in Gramp's eyes as he handed it to me. Despite my disappointment, I was curious what could be in such a small package. It was a note written in Gramp's handwriting saying I should look behind the door of their bedroom for one more gift.

All eyes were on me as I practically ran to their bedroom. Behind the door was the most beautiful rifle I had ever seen.

Later in my life there would be newer and bigger rifles with scopes, along with stories of deer, elk, caribou, bear, moose, and treks deep into wilderness areas. But for that wonderful moment on that particular Christmas Day, God answered my prayers and granted this 12-year-old the best earthly Christmas gift I could have imagined—a gift that meant the other hunters in the family would now accept me as an adult.

Christmas Day 2014 marked 60 years since I found that rifle behind my grandfather's bedroom door, but I can remember it as if it were yesterday. I thank God for giving me a grandfather who understood just what a 12-year-old boy needed. I know God was not obliged to give me that rifle. God's plans are often a lot bigger than ours. However, this time God reached down to answer a boy's prayers for the one thing he wanted most at that particular moment in his young life. Though I had prayed many, many times for a rifle, God had heard me from prayer one. He had Gramp, my parents, and my rifle all planned out for me.

The baby in the manger grew up to teach us that we can call God "our Father" in our prayers. As we study God's Word, we discover that we can count on him to answer with gifts that are good for us. He died for us to clear the way for our prayers to always be heard. He died for our sins and rose from the dead in order to save us from our sins. Now Jesus lives at God's right hand, daily adding his voice in support of all our prayers.

I was just a boy when I prayed so hard for that rifle.

What could you and I be praying for this Christmas?

Are there people you know who are living lives of despair? Perhaps you could pray that they be brought to faith.

Do you know anyone who is lonely? Maybe you can pray that he or she finds God's love.

Do you know any family members whose faith is weak? Also pray that their faith is strengthened.

Prayer is a powerful tool. Do not sell it short. God is in control and sees to it that everything works for those who love God.

Pick a person or a situation to pray for this Christmas season as earnestly as I prayed for that rifle. God already is working on the answers for your prayers just as Gramp was already working on my rifle as I was praying for it so many decades ago. Your prayers can make life more beautiful for everyone concerned if you systematically pray for others on a regular schedule. Please think about it. The Christmas season is a great time to start.

Whoever has the Son has life;
whoever does not have the Son of God does not have life.
I write these things to you who believe
in the name of the Son of God
so that you may know that you have eternal life.

*This is the confidence we have in approaching God:
that if we ask anything according to his will,
he hears us. And if we know that he hears us —
whatever we ask —
we know that we have what we asked of him.*

1 JOHN 5:12-15

TWELVE

CHRISTMAS EVE — 1922

My mother-in-law, Hilda, shared with me the following story of a Christmas Eve long ago.

Six of us, kids and adults, snuggled warmly under lap robes. The snow was too deep to use our 1916 Dodge touring car for the 8-mile trip to the church in Stuttgart, Kansas, so we were riding in the canvas-covered, two-seat surrey pulled by Jack and Jenny, our two mules. The gas lanterns on the sides of the surrey reflected off the snow, casting eerie shadows. The bells on the harnesses kept a steady rhythm as we rode through the deep snow toward town.

We arrived at the church with plenty of time to put the mules in the barn across the street from the church. Because every chair would be used for the Christmas Eve service, we had brought our own. Extras were always needed to seat the two hundred or more worshipers.

As we entered the church, we were welcomed by the warmth within. Earlier in the day, the pastor had started a fire in the huge potbellied, coal-burning stove located right in the center of the nave. We were glad that he had. The chairs were arranged in neat rows of ten on each side of the center aisle. Children under five were seated with either their fathers or their mothers. Because men and women weren't allowed to sit together, the men always sat on the right side of the nave and the women on the left. Children over five were seated in the first three rows, followed by the young people, also separated according to gender. The church was lit by a row of large two-mantle, gas lanterns that hung down from the center beam just above the heads of the taller men. Smaller kerosene lamps lined each side wall.

As a typical six-year-old, I was very excited. I had waited what seemed like forever for Christmas Eve to arrive. Now at last it was here. I was especially looking forward to the lighting of the 20-foot Christmas tree, which stood to the right side at the front of the church. Because we had no evergreens in Kansas, this tree had been brought in by train from Colorado. An assortment of colored, handblown glass balls covered the tree from top to bottom. At the end of each main branch at the front of the tree, a candleholder had been fastened. Each one held a narrow, white, 3-inch candle. A 6-inch wire with a heavy colored ball attached extended down from the candleholders. The weight of the ball kept the candles pointed upright. At the very top of the tree, a beautiful white angel reigned over the breathtaking display. Though a few other decorations had been put out, we didn't notice. All eyes were on the tree.

After we took our seats, the candles were lit. Several men with burning candles attached to the ends of sticks lit the higher candles on the tree, while some young boys carefully lit the candles they could reach. As each candle was lit, the light reflected off of the glass balls, making the tree increasingly beautiful. By the time all the candles were lit, the whole front of the church was aglow in a multitude of flickering colors. It was one of the most beautiful sights my young eyes had ever seen. Two men, seated at each side of the tree, were equipped with water buckets and long sticks with wet cloths wrapped around the end. Their job was to extinguish each candle as it burned low and to put out any fires that might have a chance to start.

The service was organized and led by our young pastor, but the children did most of the speaking—every child had a piece to say. During the service, various groups of children and young people recited the familiar account of Mary, Joseph, and the babe in the manger. I recited with a group of five other children. We children also sang several songs, and the congregation sang two as well. The singing was accompanied by a large reed pump organ, which sat to the side in the front. It was played by our cheerful organist who had to pump vigorously during the loud parts of each hymn.

As we filed out after the hour-long service was over, each child was handed a plain brown paper bag that contained nuts, candies, and a single orange. We particularly liked the orange—such things were not very common in Kansas.

On our way home in the surrey, we ate candy and talked about the tree, the service, the gifts we expected at home, and, of course, the Christmas service we would attend the next day.

When I grew up, some things were different than they had been for my mother-in-law. But it never occurred to us to miss a service either—no matter what the weather—especially during the Christmas season. Our faith in Christ made our church very much a part of everyday life for my family. Christmastime, with its special church services, was a focal point for the holiday season. I believe that's the way it should be for every Christian family today. Remember, times have changed, but the Christmas message about the Christ Child and salvation has remained constant.

Do not say, "Why were the old days better than these?"
For it is not wise to ask such questions.

ECCLESIASTES 7:10

THIRTEEN

OUR FAMILY CHRISTMAS TREE

Decorating the tree is not all fun. My wife and I haul the tree up from the basement and unpack it. We find the lights, untangle them, and check for burnt-out bulbs. Where are the extension cords? Where are the little ornament hangers? We have to move the furniture to make room. And then we have to vacuum the floor because of the dust balls that have built up under the couch all year long. The ornaments and other decorations fill up many boxes, which means many more trips up from the basement. Usually the phone interrupts us or we have to stop in the middle of decorating for some other reason, which means the big mess we have in the living room has to sit there for a while.

We have boxes of beautiful, 50-year-old, decorative glass balls of various sizes and designs. We marvel at the $1.09 price tag on a box of beautiful dime-store ornaments we bought so many years ago that are no longer available in today's stores at any price. There are many special ornaments that were given to my wife by her elementary students over her 31-year teaching career. These must all be carefully unwrapped one by one and a proper location found for each. Other ornaments with sentimental value, because they were from special people or places or have special meaning, must also be placed on the tree.

The strands of silver tinsel must be hung carefully. They cannot be allowed to touch any of the bulbs because if they do, the heat will cause them to curl up and melt.

We have so many special decorative items collected through the years. Each piece is specially placed as we remember from whom we received it or where we purchased it.

It usually takes us most of a day from the time we start to the time we add the finishing touch: the angel that sits on the very top of the tree. By then the darkness of the winter evening has closed in around our home, and Ruth and I are both so tired that we are no longer convinced putting up the tree was really worth the trouble.

After adding a few sticks of wood to the fire, we collapse into our easy chairs by the fireplace and rest for a few moments. Then, somewhat refreshed, we plug in the lights. As if by magic, the tree, the living room, and our attitudes are transformed. Now the crèche is lit on the dining room counter. Soon the packages will be wrapped and placed with care under the tree. Soon our Yule log will be burning in the fireplace. Soon Christmas Eve will be upon us and it will be time to leave to see this year's program at church. Once again the house glows with warmth and beauty befitting the One whose birthday the tree celebrates. It is no longer an everyday living room. Problems we encountered putting up the tree are forgotten. Ruth and I embrace. We recall memories of past Christmases. We remember those warm Christmas gatherings. Sometimes we drove hundreds of miles through snow and rain to join in the hustle and bustle of a house full of extended family and friends singing carols, talking about the good old days, opening gifts, and eating. Remember the special foods, candies, cookies, and desserts our mothers and grandmothers used to cook? We can almost taste them now. We remember loved ones who are no longer with us and share stories again about the special ornaments picked by my son, as well as others received from relatives, students, and close friends. As we look at the angel at the top of our tree, we are reminded once again that the real meaning of Christmas is the Christ Child lying in a manger under a star-filled sky. As the sounds of Christmas carols come from our stereo, we quietly reflect upon the true purpose behind the tree and other decorations. We always find reviewing the Christmas story to be a humbling experience.

Sometimes, as Ruth and I admire a beautiful Christmas tree in another family's window, we start to think about what that tree might say if it could talk.

O Christmas tree, shining brightly on this dark December night, tell us about yourself:

I represent the story of the birth of the Son of God.

At my top a large angel stands ready again to tell the shepherds in their fields, "A Savior has been born to you." Each of my lights is like the Christmas star, placed in the sky to show the far-distant nations that their Savior had been born. The colored ornaments as well as my fragrant branches remind people of the very first Christmas gifts the wise men brought on bended knee to the baby Jesus. My tinsel sparkles in the light as God's child would grow up to shine with heavenly glory, brighter than the noonday sun. I also have special decorations, some made by hand and some bought at stores by the family who owns me. All these bring back wonderful memories of Christmases past. My branches stretch out wide to gather in the lost with the gospel message of hope and salvation. The garland ropes that surround me remind others of the ties all Christians have with this joyous, holy celebration that comes but once a year.

I have been lovingly placed in the front window to broadcast this story of the gift of God's love from my Christian family to others: "God so loved the world that he gave his one and only Son, that whoever believes in him shall not perish but have eternal life" (John 3:16).

I guess it is worth all the trouble after all, to put up our family Christmas tree. 🌿

On the mountain heights of Israel I will plant it;
it will produce branches and bear fruit
and become a splendid cedar.

EZEKIEL 17:23

FOURTEEN

STABLE

In another book, I have told how my grandfather Lloyd M. Holley showed the spirit of Christmas all year long. However, I did not tell the whole story.

Sadly, Gramp's first wife, Marion Lowry Holley, took her own life when I was 15 years old and a sophomore in high school. It was August 17, 1958. Because I was old enough to ask questions, Dad did his best to explain to me what had happened. He said Gramp was having breakfast at the little table in their kitchen when he heard the gunshot. She had been ill with stomach and heart problems, which were compounded by bouts of depression. For months Gramp had rarely left her side. His loaded .22 caliber pistol was always kept in his bedroom dresser. My grandfather never talked about her suicide. However, years later, when he and I were having dinner in a restaurant discussing how my first wife too was struggling with depression, Gramp did say, "I don't have to go back too far to have my own regrets."

Shortly after Marion's death, Gramp tore down the house where she had died. Most of the time he lived near us in a little house trailer parked under the large oak trees near our home. Much of the time he ate with us. He hired me to help get his old house torn down. A year or so later he built a new house near where the old one had been.

Not long after that, on August 19, 1960, he married Margaret Mosbarger. We always called her "Grandma Margaret." She was good for him. She gave Gramp a chance to hunt and travel like he never could before. But she did more than that.

When a tragedy comes into a person's life, it can be hard to trust God, to keep a childlike faith in him. In the back of a person's head there can be a voice that says, "God has let a whole lot of hurt into my life already. What problem is he going to send next? Will it be even worse?" A hurt has to be pretty bad to make a person want to tear down their own house. Grandma Margaret seemed to be God's way of keeping Gramp close to him, close to his Word; keeping Gramp's faith stable; and keeping him from brooding over his own regrets. Grandma Margaret encouraged him to be more involved in church and in doing things for people.

He was a role model for Christianity. He and Margaret were in church almost every Sunday. They always sat next to the aisle in the last pew on the right-hand side of the church. He regularly helped at church picnics, and on one occasion, he went on a weeklong trip to work in a mission field. In 1960 I went with him on that mission trip to work in a Navajo school in Tuba City, Arizona. We painted, cleaned, did yard work and carpentry, and generally helped out any way we could. We enjoyed working hard for the Lord. Whenever I was too critical of our church, Gramp got after me. If he thought I was speaking out of line, he did not hesitate to say so.

He was always willing to offer someone help if they needed it. I remember one day around Christmastime when Gramp came home and told Margaret that a family he knew was short on food. "Why! Go take them some. Don't worry about it," she told him. "They need it, and you should go and help them." He did. He took them about six huge bags of groceries, a turkey, and some canned ham. There were about 13 kids at that house. Not that Gramp ever told me anything about it: I had to find out from Margaret later. From that point on, Christmas to him was all year-round. If he could help or counsel someone, he would do it in a heartbeat. Maybe the hurt he had been through made him quicker to take to heart the hurts of others.

Once when I was working on his ranch to get money for the next year's college tuition, Gramp came by and said, "I have a set of new tires for your car. I'll tell you where to go to get them put on." He helped me again by trading my 1953 Mercury for a 1955 Chevrolet he found on a local car dealer's lot. He paid the price difference. He felt it was a safer car for me to take 1,200 miles away from home, when I went off to Whitworth College in Spokane, Washington. I loved that car with its four-barrel carburetor. I wish I still had it.

Later he paid for about half of the first year's college tuition for my wife. Gramp and Margaret were the only ones who made the long trip to attend the ceremony when both of us walked across the stage and received our teaching degrees. That weekend I told him about a family of five living near us. The father had also been attending college. They were really strapped for money and the father needed $100 to graduate. Gramp gave a local church $100 to take to them. I remember how the mother in the family came over to our apartment saying, "Some nice person at church gave us a hundred dollars." She was almost walking on air. I passed that moment along to Gramp.

Following the graduation, he and Margaret also helped us pack our few possessions in a small U-Haul trailer and make the move to Yakima to start my teaching career. I think my wife and I had about $50 to our name for gas and food. I guess Gramp noticed how few pieces of furniture we had, because when we arrived at the duplex we had rented, we found a surprise. Gramp and Margaret had gotten there ahead of us. They had arranged for a kitchen table with four chairs, along with a washer, to be delivered to our duplex. My wife and I thought Christmas had arrived early. I knew I was blessed to have people like Gramp and Margaret helping us get a start in life.

I wasn't the only one thankful for their generosity. Family members who were sick or in a hard spot often saw Gramp's helping hand. I have seen him slip money to the wife of a wounded veteran who was out of work and was too proud to take help himself.

It wasn't that Gramp was a millionaire. However, God had blessed him, and he knew it. He wanted, in turn, to be a blessing to others. He took my brother deer hunting in Utah, which my brother has never forgotten. He also funded deer hunts with his son Bernard and his son-in-law Kenneth. They went to Utah and Colorado and had some great times.

When he was not working, traveling, or hunting, he loved to make things.

One Christmas, he gave me a beautiful footlocker-sized wooden chest he had built from finished lumber. It has a tray inside that slides back and forth and my name wood-burned into the top. Another year at Christmas he made another chest, just like mine, for my son, Greg, with his name on top. They are beautiful pieces of work.

In December 1967, a medium-sized, handmade, wooden crate arrived in the mail. That crate itself was a special piece of work. When I pried it open, I found a miniature, handmade stable to be used with a nativity set. Each piece of wood had been carefully cut, stained with dark walnut stain, and lovingly nailed in its proper place. The design was ingenious. It has one light bulb inside, in just the right spot. The bulb shines up through a hole in the roof, illuminating a white metal star, representing the one the wise men followed. At the same time, the bulb shines downward onto the baby Jesus. That stable with its manger scene is still the first Christmas decoration I put up each year and the last one I take down. Over the years, Gramp quietly made and gave away 136 of those stables. In many homes, the little lights Gramp wired into those stables continue to shine on the One whose love keeps the spirit of Christmas going.

I cannot imagine the pain Gramp felt that morning when he went to the bedroom and saw Grandma Marion's body. I had mixed feelings about whether to even tell that part of the story. But this tragedy was a turning point in Gramp's life. God was there for him through it all and, if anything, used it to make Gramp's faith stronger than ever. He was a Christian man who finished only two years of high school, but influenced and was a blessing to many, many people in my family, home church, and community. I believe he demonstrated the spirit of Christmas all year round.

To him, Jesus wasn't just a baby *in a stable* long ago. Jesus was the unfailing friend who had *kept him stable* in times of deepest sorrow. With a little encouragement from Grandma Margaret, Gramp made a point to be a friend to other people who were struggling, thereby showing them what Jesus meant to him.

What has Jesus, born at Christmas, meant to you?

> *It is God who arms me with strength*
> *and keeps my way secure.*
>
> **PSALM 18:32**

FIFTEEN

MAYONNAISE AND KETCHUP

Each Christmas season a needy family from the community is assigned to our church. We receive information about the names, ages, and needs of the various children in the family. We try very hard to make sure the children get something for fun and several things they really need such as shoes or coats. We also collect cans and boxes of nonperishable foods. We try to provide plenty of food for several meals in addition to a big Christmas feast.

I have to admit this is one of my pet projects each year. I feel strongly that helping others is one of the ways we reflect the love of Jesus to others. Jesus often spoke of concern for the needy. "When you give a luncheon or dinner, do not invite your friends, your brothers or sisters, your relatives, or your rich neighbors; if you do, they may invite you back and so you will be repaid. But when you give a banquet, invite the poor, the crippled, the lame, the blind, and you will be blessed. Although they cannot repay you, you will be repaid at the resurrection of the righteous" (Luke 14:12-14). In fact, in Matthew 25:40, Jesus revealed an astounding truth: "Truly I tell you, whatever you did for one of the least of these brothers and sisters of mine, you did for me." Many people need a hand up. I needed one when I went through college. Without the work, money, and encouragement several Christians gave me, I would not have made it.

On several occasions, my wife and I have had the privilege of accompanying the pastor when he delivers the gifts. Over the years, the needs of some families have been more evident than others. But one delivery in particular stands out in my mind.

Our assigned family that year included three children. Because of an accident, the father had been unable to work for over a year. The mother had a job, but it was difficult for her to make ends meet. We gathered the boxes of presents our youth group had wrapped, as well as boxes of food items, and called to make sure someone would be home.

With the presents in the back of my pickup, we arrived at the address we had been given. The mother answered the door and invited us to come in. After we introduced ourselves, we presented her with a letter explaining that the gifts were from Redeemer Evangelical Lutheran Church. We also explained a little about what we believe.

The clean living room was decorated with just a few pictures on the wall. A set of crutches stood in one corner. Though it was less than a week before Christmas, the small Christmas tree on the table held only a few handmade decorations. The few presents already under the tree appeared to be handmade. The mother pointed to the portraits of the three children on top of an old television set and proudly told us a little about each of the three boys.

As we placed our presents around the tree, I noticed that the mother was looking at the boxes of food. We began to tell her what was in some of those boxes.

Up to that point I had been fine. The introductions, gift presentation, and discussion about the family hadn't bothered me. However, as we put the last gifts under the tree, she again looked wistfully at the boxes of food. I will never forget what she said as she turned toward us. "I think all I have left in the refrigerator is some mayonnaise and ketchup." Until she said those words, I had not fully recognized their plight. However, as she spoke, something got in my eyes, a lump formed in my throat, and I thanked God our church people had been so generous.

Through James, God tells us "to look after orphans and widows in their distress" (James 1:27). Should Christians be involved in helping the needy? Should we help even more than we do? Should Christians be concerned about the material as well as the spiritual welfare of others? Before you answer, check your refrigerator. How are you fixed for mayonnaise and ketchup?

Religion that God our Father accepts
as pure and faultless is this:
to look after orphans and widows in their distress
and to keep oneself from being polluted by the world.

JAMES 1:27

SIXTEEN

CHRISTMAS WITHOUT THE CLASSICS

One of my favorite things about Christmas is the music. Ruth thinks I am a little crazy because I start listening to Christmas music as early as October and occasionally listen to an album of Christmas music other times during the year. No music is quite like the beautiful songs associated with Christmas, which express the joy at the birth of the Christ Child. Christmas songs put a wonderful, warm feeling into my heart, even if I hear them in July.

What would Christmas be without music? The other day Ruth and I were discussing that very question. I had made the statement, "Christmas must have surely been different before 1930 because so many of the Christmas classics were written since that year."

"Imagine," I said, without giving a lot of thought to what I was saying, "Christmas without 'Rudolph' (1949), 'White Christmas' (1940), 'Here Comes Santa Claus' (1947), 'The Little Drummer Boy' (1941), 'Sleigh Ride' (1948), 'Santa Claus Is Coming to Town'

(1934), 'Silver Bells' (1950), 'Frosty the Snowman' (1950), 'The Christmas Song' (1944), 'Home for the Holidays' (1954), 'Winter Wonderland' (1934), or 'Grandma Got Run Over by a Reindeer' (1979)."

My wife sat thoughtfully for a moment and then quietly said, "Maybe back then they concentrated more on going to church and singing songs about the baby Jesus to celebrate Christmas."

That comment made me stop and rethink what I had just said. Ruth was right to notice that most of the songs I had mentioned had nothing to do with Jesus. I suppose in the days before radio, movies, and TV, people learned Christmas songs from a hymnal or from their parents. Unfortunately, there is less and less of that these days.

I love secular Christmas music and have an extensive collection of albums to prove it. Songs that celebrate winter landscapes, fun in the snow, romance by the fireplace, or a make-believe character have nothing wrong with them. "Everything God created is good, and nothing is to be rejected if it is received with thanksgiving" (1 Timothy 4:4). Songs like these can remind us to appreciate and be thankful for the beauty that is all around us at Christmastime.

But there is special joy in listening to the wonderful Christmas songs about *Jesus*. Let's get more of those songs out during the Christmas season. What a blessing they can be for all who hear them! When someone comments on the music you're playing, you get a chance to say what the Savior's birth means to you. From there, you are but one small step away from asking that individual to come with you to some Christmas activity at church. Do it! Help put a Christmas song in that person's heart that tells of Jesus and his gospel. He or she will thank you later!

Soon Christmas will be upon us again. People around the world will begin singing their favorite Christmas songs. Let us offer this prayer for them: "Lord, help the people who sing those glorious Christmas songs about the birth of our Savior to listen carefully to the words they are saying. Help people everywhere to recognize and take to heart the glorious story of Jesus' birth and the gospel message these songs portray, so all may be saved."

Let us pray for this to happen with all our hearts! ※

Sing we now of Christmas, Noel, sing we here!
Hear our grateful praises to the babe so dear.

FROM THE TRADITIONAL FRENCH CAROL, "NOEL NOUVELET."

SEVENTEEN

A HUMBLE CORONATION

I was nine years old when King George VI of England, the beloved king who had led his country through the horrors of World War II, passed away on February 6, 1952. My memories of events from those long ago times are not all that good, so a computer was used to find the correct date and much of the detail in this story.

However, I didn't have to look up the date when, after 16 months of preparations, King George's daughter was crowned Queen Elizabeth II. I remember June 2, 1953, well. Our family had no television at that time, but my father's parents had bought one of the first black and white TV sets in our neighborhood. Even though my grandparents were gone on an extended trip to New England, our family was allowed to go over to their house to watch the Queen's coronation. It was the first TV broadcast I had ever seen.

The TV stations could not show it live, as they can easily do now. But the metal film canisters were flown across the Atlantic and then, as fast as possible, to the major cities in the United States. In this way many people all around the United States were able to watch the coronation on the same evening.

People who know me personally might think my first TV show would have been a western, but that was not the case. All my adult life I have remembered sitting in my grandparents' living room watching the crowning of Queen Elizabeth with my parents and my little brother and sister. The coronation was very impressive to me because of the newness of television and the majestic ceremony. I had never seen anything with that much pomp and circumstance. As I write this, a little over six decades have passed, and it is still a vivid memory.

How does the beginning of the reign of Jesus, our King, compare to Her Majesty's coronation?

Her Majesty arrived in a golden coach, two centuries old, drawn by eight Windsor Greys in gold and crimson harnesses. Our King arrived in the womb of a virgin living in poverty. When he was born, he was laid in the straw of a feeding trough for animals because there had been no room for the family to stay in the local inn.

Her Majesty's procession passed through the streets of London with thousands of soldiers, sailors, and airmen. Grenadiers and other red-clad guards in bearskin hats escorted her. Our King Jesus' only guard was his stepfather, Joseph, a simple carpenter. Jesus' safety was so much in doubt that he and his family would soon flee all the way to Egypt, where the long arm of King Herod and his pitiless soldiers could no longer reach them.

Six maidens carried Elizabeth's majestic train. Her embroidered silk gown sparkled with jewels. She was given a cape and sash of golden cloth as well as gold bracelets and a ring covered in rubies. Our King Jesus was wrapped in torn strips of cloth. We are left to wonder how long it was before the gifts of the wise men were spent or bartered to pay for lodging and food on the trip to Egypt.

Bells rang for Her Majesty Elizabeth II. Gunfire saluted her. Crowds cheered for hours. A choir of hundreds sang at her service. Our King Jesus had an angel choir, but they sang out in the fields for the benefit of the lowly shepherds, too far away for Jesus to hear them in Bethlehem.

Bishops and dukes bowed and removed their crowns before Her Majesty the Queen. They pledged their loyalty and earthly worship. Shepherds, who rarely bathed and smelled of the livestock they tended, came as they were from the hills to bow before Jesus and worship him as their Savior and King.

Inscribed in the lectern at Westminster Abbey are the words "Attempt Great Things for God." Baby Jesus, our King, would grow up to *accomplish*, not just attempt, great things for God such as performing miracles of healing, dying for the world's sins, and conquering death on Easter morning.

Her Majesty Elizabeth II insisted that the service held in Westminster Abbey be filmed for posterity. Only one part was deemed too holy to be allowed on film. The Archbishop of Canterbury was to anoint her forehead with precious oil. To hide this anointing from the cameras, four Knights of the Garter held a canopy of golden silk over the Queen. Our King Jesus was anointed also. The Holy Spirit did this at his conception, while he was still in Mary's womb. No one saw the ceremony and no camera filmed it. The angel told the shepherds, "Unto you is born this day in the city of David a Saviour, which is Christ the Lord" (Luke 2:11 KJV). This quote from God's Word makes it clear that at his birth he was the Christ, the Anointed One.

One of the many golden items Her Majesty was given at her coronation was the Sovereign Orb, a jeweled golden globe with a golden cross atop it. As the Archbishop gave it to her, he told her to "remember that the whole world is subject to the power and empire of Christ our Redeemer." As Baby Jesus lay in his manger bed, it did not seem like he had power or an empire. As he nursed at Mary's breast, it did not look like the whole world was subject to him. Nothing about his lowly birth suggested that centuries later, rulers like Elizabeth II would need to be reminded that they too are subject to Jesus.

You and I need to be reminded as well. The Savior we thank God for at Christmas has power over everything in this whole wide world. God's Word tells us he has his eye on every sparrow and each hair on our heads. Let us remember that he is truly in the room with us each day as we bow our heads in prayer, placing our troubles, worries, and questions into his hands. As Christians, we can show this faith by boldly "attempting great things for God" as we go through our everyday activities. Let us reflect the joy we have in our hearts because Jesus is our Savior and King. One day, we will leave this world. We look forward to that day because we know through our faith and belief in Christ that when this world ends for us, it will be *our* coronation day in heaven. All our worries, pain, and suffering will be gone, and we will live forever with Jesus in heaven as he promises in the Bible. Praise the Lord!

As the Archbishop told Queen Elizabeth, "Remember that the whole world is subject to the power and empire of Christ our Redeemer."

He will be great and will be called the Son of the Most High. The Lord God will give him the throne of his father David, and he will reign over Jacob's descendants forever; his kingdom will never end.

LUKE 1:32,33

And it came to pass in those days, that there went out a decree from Caesar Augustus that all the world should be taxed. (And this taxing was first made when Cyrenius was governor of Syria.) And all went to be taxed, every one into his own city. And Joseph also went up from Galilee, out of the city of Nazareth, into Judaea, unto the city of David, which is called Bethlehem; (because he was of the house and lineage of David:) To be taxed with Mary his espoused wife, being great with child. And so it was, that, while they were there, the days were accomplished that she should be delivered. And she brought forth her firstborn son, and wrapped him in swaddling clothes, and laid him in a manger; because there was no room for them in the inn.

And there were in the same country shepherds abiding in the field, keeping watch over their flock by night. And, lo, the angel of the Lord came upon them, and the glory of the Lord shone round about them: and they were sore afraid. And the angel said unto them, Fear not: for, behold, I bring you good tidings of great joy, which shall be to all people. For unto you is born this day in the city of David a Saviour, which is Christ the Lord. And this shall be a sign unto you; Ye shall find the babe wrapped in swaddling clothes, lying in a manger. And suddenly there was with the angel a multitude of the heavenly host praising God, and saying, Glory to God in the highest, and on earth peace, good will toward men. And it came to pass, as the angels were gone away from them into heaven, the shepherds said one to another, Let us now go even unto Bethlehem, and see this thing which is come to pass, which the Lord hath made known unto us. And they came with haste, and found Mary, and Joseph, and the babe lying in a manger. And when they had seen it, they made known abroad the saying which was told them concerning this child. And all they that heard it wondered at those things which were told them by the shepherds. But Mary kept all these things, and pondered them in her heart. And the shepherds returned, glorifying and praising God for all the things that they had heard and seen, as it was told unto them. (Luke 2:1-20 KJV) 🌿